LOS ANGELES CONFIDENTIAL

HIDDEN GEMS LOVED BY LOCALS

WRITTEN BY ANDRÉ MICHEL
PHOTOGRAPHED BY PIA RIVEROLA
ILLUSTRATED BY CLARA MARI

JONGLEZ PUBLISHING

Travel guides

Hotel California
HOLLYWOOD

*"WHEN PEOPLE CRITICIZE LA,
THEY ARE USUALLY AFRAID
OF EXPLORING,
AND PROBABLY TOO USED
TO EASY CITIES
WHERE YOU DON'T HAVE TO FIGHT
TO FIND BEAUTIFUL THINGS."*

MOBY

WHAT YOU WON'T FIND IN THIS GUIDE

- Weather information
  (320 days of sunshine a year is enough)
- Tips on how to skip the lines at Disneyland Park
  (hint: you have to pay a lot of money)
- A map with public transportation
  (very limited anyway)

WHAT YOU WILL FIND IN THIS GUIDE

- Where to drink the oldest cocktail in Hollywood
- How to order your burger the right way
- How to relax from traffic at a gigantic 24/7 Korean spa
- Where chefs buy their groceries
- A secret museum in Holmby Hills
- Where to watch movies from Tarantino's personal collection
- The perfect Californian house to photograph
- A much-loved garden

Los Angeles is a city of clichés. Many first-time visitors fall for tourist traps like the Hollywood Walk of Fame and the Venice Boardwalk. Instead of finding glamour, they will soon be disappointed by the shabby streets, maddening crowds and overpriced attractions. Add to that the long distances and crazy traffic and they will think they've made a mistake in coming. However, you are different. By opening this book and reading these lines, you have already proved that you have the right mindset for this town. In Los Angeles, you have to possess an explorer's mindset to fully enjoy this sprawling urban jungle. When planning your stay, we recommend you stick to one area per day and do things that are close together. With its 20 million inhabitants, this town is massive.

We have been searching for gems in this city for a decade and this is a collection of some of the experiences that made us love Los Angeles. We are excited to share them with you.

We hope you enjoy our discoveries!

André Michel, author

André Michel

When the question of who should write "Soul of Los Angeles", there was no doubt: either André Michel would do it, or there would be no guide.

André is one of those rare characters who are as crazy, vibrant, and excessive as LA itself. Back when I met him, he was working for Apple while simultaneously writing for magazines like *Purple* and *Apartamento*, organizing one of the most popular dinners in LA (the famous Suicide Sommelier Series), participating in architecture debates at night, and above all testing every – and I mean absolutely every – eatery in town, from the little pizza shop in El Sereno to the biggest restaurant in West Hollywood.

Thank you, André, for sharing your secret Los Angeles with us ... And thank you to your two sidekicks, Pia and Clara, for having captured the soul of the city so well in their photographs and drawings.

Fany Péchiodat

SYMBOLS OF

LOS ANGELES

Free

0 to $20

$20 and more

First come
first served

Book ahead

"This is so LA"

Opening times often vary,
so we recommend checking them directly
on the website of the place you plan to visit.

30 EXPERIENCES

01. The post-modern lunch
02. The craziest LA museum is in a mansion
03. The hike with a view where people get dressed up
04. Cocktail with Hollywood royalty
05. Where to watch Tarantino's movie collection
06. Picnic and concert under the stars
07. The obsessive antiques dealer
08. The restaurant – bakery – cafe that will make you wish you lived in Venice
09. The perfect Californian home
10. Elvis and George Harrison's peaceful getaway
11. Drink the oldest Martini in Hollywood
12. The restaurant that invented a dish that has been copied everywhere – even in China
13. The pole-dancing club where Courtney Love met Kurt Cobain
14. The shop for movie fans
15. Wander around a breathtaking garden
16. Eat your burger the Californian way
17. The secret Malibu Beach you can only access at low tide
18. Shop for your produce with local chefs
19. The best sushi in town in an unusual spot
20. The hotel next to your surf spot
21. The jazz bar created by music royalty
22. James Turrell's gallery
23. The shop that embodies the Venice Beach lifestyle
24. Jonathan Gold's favorite taco truck
25. The Korean spa open 24/7
26. The building movie star
27. The breakfast place with the famous take-home jam
28. The smallest comedy club for the biggest acts
29. Buy a vinyl and a dress from the same year
30. Enjoy thai "drink food" paired with rare natural wines

OLLYWOOD
21
6
3
9
11
13
14
4
7
16
30
29
15
2
28
5
27
12
22
25
26
19
1
24
8
20
8
23

DESTROYER

#01

THE POST-MODERN **LUNCH**

Vespertine may be the most talked-about restaurant" in Los Angeles, but at $330 per person (excluding drinks), you could be forgiven for giving it a pass.

But if you're still determined to sample the superb cuisine of its chef, Jordan Kahn, you're in luck. He has just opened an even more adorable little gem right across the street: Destroyer.

Open every day for breakfast and lunch, Destroyer offers exquisitely delicious bowls of food and dishes served on custom-made ceramics.

DESTROYER
3578 HAYDEN AVE, CULVER CITY,
LOS ANGELES, CA 90232

No reservations, walk-in only	+1 (310) 360-3860	destroyer.la Instagram: @destroyer.la

#02

THE CRAZIEST LA MUSEUM **IS IN A MANSION**

One of our favorite gems is also one of LA's best-kept secrets. The Weisman Art Foundation is a major museum in Holmby Hills that most city residents haven't even heard of. It includes at least one piece by every major artist of the late 20th century (Picasso, Bacon, Hockney, Magritte, de Kooning, Rothko, Warhol, Stella and more).

Frederick Weisman was an entrepreneur born in Minnesota and raised in Los Angeles, where he began collecting art in the mid-1950s with Marcia Simon Weisman. He later married Billie Milam, a former conservator at the Los Angeles County Museum of Art (LACMA) and the Getty Museum, and together they amassed one of the most beautiful post-war art collections in the country

The best and most unique part of this foundation is how the artwork is displayed. Visitors get to see the art in the Weismans' home, just as the couple lived in it from 1982 to 1992. The domestic setting, which includes original furniture, is a pleasant change from the starker setting of a museum gallery. For that reason, the only way to visit is to contact the foundation in advance to book a tour.

FREDERICK R. WEISMAN ART FOUNDATION

FREE

They will give you the address upon reservation (Holmby Hills)

Mandatory free advanced reservation by email or phone:
tours@weismanfoundation.org
+1 (310) 277-5321
Instagram: @weismanartfoundation

© PIA RIVEROLA - FREDERICK R. WEISMAN ART FOUNDATION. LOS ANGELES

© PIA RIVEROLA - FREDERICK R. WEISMAN ART FOUNDATION, LOS ANGELES

THE HIKE WITH A VIEW **WHERE PEOPLE GET DRESSED UP**

The landscape surrounding Los Angeles is stunning and varies widely, from ocean to desert and hills around Malibu and Hollywood. These hills afford the opportunity for many hikes (you can find them on the app AllTrails) but Runyon Canyon is the most quintessentially LA of them all. Is it popular because of its central location adjacent to Hollywood which provides a good workout for aspiring actors and actresses? Or because of its stunning views of the city? Or maybe because some parts are pet friendly? Probably all of the above.

Once on the hike, don't be surprised if it looks like an athleisure catwalk, with social media influencers donning makeup and expensive gear to share with passersby and their followers. For some "hikers", the selfie may be more important than the actual hike.

RUNYON CANYON PARK
2000 N. FULLER AVE,
LOS ANGELES, CA 90046

Dawn to dusk seven days a week

© SUNSET TOWER HOTEL

#04

COCKTAILS WITH HOLLYWOOD ROYALTY

The Tower Bar is one of America's most beautiful restaurants. Order a cocktail and some nibbles and sink into the dimly lit atmosphere – it's pure bliss.

Tucked inside the Sunset Tower Hotel, the restaurant feels frozen in 1931, the year this Art Deco building was completed. The hotel itself only opened in 2006, though, after Jeff Klein bought and transformed what had once been a residential building, home to John Wayne, Howard Hughes and Frank Sinatra.

Klein's brilliant architect, the late Paul Fortune, turned it into an unmissable destination with the perfect restaurant design: white tablecloths, a jazz band, a fireplace, candles in place of chandeliers – and impeccable service.

Glance around the room: those signed portraits on the walls belong to actors who never quite made it. But here in the dining room, everyone who matters in Hollywood has shown up – gossiping, flirting and whispering about the industry's future.

THE TOWER BAR AT SUNSET TOWER HOTEL
8358 SUNSET BLVD,
WEST HOLLYWOOD, CA 90069

+1 (323) 848-6677
Instagram: @sunset_tower

sunsettowerhotel.com/restaurants-and-bar/tower-bar

WHERE TO WATCH **TARANTINO'S MOVIE COLLECTION**

Before he became famous, Tarantino was just an ordinary staff member at a video store. An obsessive film buff, over time he amassed one of the world's biggest film collections.

What's more, because he hates digital screenings, which he blames for killing "what [he] knew as cinema," he decided to save the last movie theater in LA that was still showing movies the old-school way, on 35mm analog film.

Now the owner of the New Beverly Cinema, Tarantino has made his vast collection available to the public. You can come here to catch all kinds of movies (spaghetti westerns, blaxploitation, film noir, vintage comedies), including Tarantino's own films, which are screened every Friday at midnight.

The prices are very affordable, just like back in the day. You can even watch a double feature (two movies shown back-to-back) for the price of one.

NEW BEVERLY CINEMA
7165 BEVERLY BLVD,
LOS ANGELES, CA 90036

Instagram: @newbeverly

See website for updated calendar and tickets: thenewbev.com

EXIT
Pulp Fiction
Quentin Tarantino

Coca-Cola
GEN ADMISSION
$10.00
SENIOR CHILD
$6.00
MIDNIGHT
$10.00
MATINEE
$6.00

#06

PICNIC AND CONCERT **UNDER THE STARS**

If you have to choose only one concert venue during your visit, this is the one. Built into the side of the Hollywood Hills, this outdoor venue is only open from Spring to October. There is nothing like seeing a show by your favorite artist or your favorite genre – from classical to pop – in this magical setting, surrounded by the hills and lit by the moon.

Come early, bring a picnic and a bottle of wine so you can eat before the main show starts.

This place brings together families, lovers and friends from every generation. It's an LA attraction that never disappoints.

HOLLYWOOD BOWL
2301 N HIGHLAND AVE,
LOS ANGELES, CA 90068

Shows most days of the week in spring and summer

See website for updated calendar and reservations: hollywoodbowl.com

#07

THE OBSESSIVE **ANTIQUES DEALER**

Think of this spot as a sort of epicenter for high-quality furniture and design. Joel Chen, the son of a Chinese immigrant jeweler, started the business 40 years ago.

One of the most important antiques dealers in the world, he has no fewer than three massive, multi-floor showrooms to exhibit his 50,000+ piece collection, which ranges from rare Chinese antiques to cutting-edge modern furniture.

Chen is an expert on the widely influential married designer couple Eames – known for their industrial esthetic and celebrated for their iconic chairs – but also has an extensive collection of work by designers from around the world, such as Prouve, Sottsass, Kjaerholm, and Judd. It helps to call ahead prior to a visit.

JF CHEN
1000 N HIGHLAND AVE,
LOS ANGELES, CA 90038

By appointment only	+1 (323) 463-4603	Instagram: @jfchenantiques

– JOEL CHEN –

JF Chen was created by Joel Chen, one of the most important antiques dealers in the world and an expert on the work of designers Charles and Ray Eames.

How did you become an antiques dealer?

I came from England originally and my parents emigrated in Los Angeles in the 1970s. My father was a jeweler downtown, I was working for him and I did not like it. It was a cutting-throat business. I was in my twenties, driving on Melrose one day, and I saw a store window with beautiful Chinese antiques. I rang the bell many times, and the guy would not open to me. He finally did and said it was for "trade only". I got mad, I thought it was racial because I was Asian. I went back to my father and said I would open an antiques store because this guy would not let him in. I borrowed $6,000 from the bank, co-signed by my father. I went to Hong Kong and bought a whole container of junk – I did not have a clue! I started selling it. And then more containers followed. There was no internet then,

When they enter the space, some people are overwhelmed

so after that I flew to get antiques all throughout Europe, which was opening up after the Berlin Wall fell.

What about California and design?

When I started, I heard things like "California is the armpits of the world." It changed a lot with lots of museums opening recently such as The Broad. It took a long time for it to change. I did an Ettore Sottsass show, then a Charles and Ray Eames show. I also recently did a show with Daft Punk making furniture.

What is the best way to start your furniture/design collection?

The old story was flying here, flying there. Now with the internet, it changed everything, no need to travel anymore. There are auctions constantly!
Six auctions a day. Go through everything and try to pick up what you like. Forget about Jean Prouvé, Charlotte Perriand: don't do it.
Just look for the new talents or the "sleeper" talents that are still affordable from all over the world, and go f
or it! Now we're very mid-century and I see antiques are coming back: Louis XVI, Louis XV, this is very elegant.

© BARRY SCHWARTZ

#08

THE RESTAURANT – BAKERY – CAFE **THAT WILL MAKE YOU WISH YOU LIVED IN VENICE BEACH**

The restaurant Gjusta never sleeps. At night, they bake hundreds of loaves of bread, and during the day, they serve from their deli counter some of the most delicious breakfasts, lunches, and dinners in town – and snacks too, if you're still hungry.

With 130 employees, everything they offer is made from scratch and on site: bread, pastries, desserts, salads, breakfasts, pizzas, sandwiches, pasta, juices, coffees, and so forth ...

Try to go at off-peak times, so that you can avoid the crowd that is growing bigger and bigger as word gets out.

GJUSTA
320 SUNSET AVE,
VENICE, CA 90291

No reservations, walk-in only
+1 (310) 314-0320

Instagram: @gjustabakery

gjusta.com

Gjusta
GOODS
OPEN DAILY

#09

THE PERFECT **CALIFORNIAN HOME**

There it is, the picture-perfect house ... the one that made everyone on the planet want a house with a pool in the Los Angeles hills: The Stahl House. The photographer of the house, Julius Shulman, probably didn't realize the impact his images would ultimately have on modern design.

When you're actually there, the Stahl House is smaller than you may have expected. Nonetheless, Case Study House #22, designed by Pierre Koenig, is still incredibly photogenic sixty years after its construction. It was made for a family with "champagne tastes and a beer budget," using inexpensive materials of the time.

Booking in advance on the website weeks ahead is essential if you want to visit the house during the day or during the coveted sunset hours.

STAHL HOUSE
CASE STUDY HOUSE #22

Afternoon and evening tour	Mandatory paid advanced reservation on their website: stahlhouse.com	They will give you the address upon reservation (West Hollywood)

THE ICONIC **ARCHITECTURE**

WALT DISNEY HALL

FRANK GEHRY - 2003

ENNIS HOUSE

FRANK LLOYD WRIGHT - 1924

GRIFFITH OBSERVATORY

JOHN C. AUSTIN - 1935

SHEATS GOLDSTEIN RESIDENCE

JOHN LAUTNER - 1963

RANDY'S DONUTS

HENRY J. GOODWIN - 1953

#10

ELVIS AND GEORGE HARRISON'S **PEACEFUL GETAWAY**

The Self-Realization Fellowship Lake Shrine Temple is an exceptional place to escape the hubbub of the city and just spend some time with yourself (so therapeutic sometimes!).

It was founded by Yogi Paramahansa Yogananda, who is credited with introducing meditation and yoga to the Western world and counted Steve Jobs as one of his prominent followers.

This place is a garden surrounding a lake with many animals: swans, ducks, koi fish, and turtles. The center's spiritual crown jewel is its outdoor shrine, the Mahatma Gandhi World Peace Memorial, where a thousand-year-old Chinese stone sarcophagus holds some of Gandhi's ashes.

Elvis Presley was a regular, and George Harrison and Tom Petty loved the center so much, their funerals were held here, 16 years apart.

SELF-REALIZATION FELLOWSHIP LAKE SHRINE TEMPLE
17190 SUNSET BLVD,
PACIFIC PALISADES, CA 90272

+1 (310) 454-4114

Free reservation required:
lakeshrine.org

#11

DRINK THE OLDEST MARTINI **IN HOLLYWOOD**

On a first trip to LA, many tourists go to Hollywood Boulevard expecting glitz and glamor, but are disappointed by the dirty streets, trashy tourist traps, and soulless big chain stores.

Yet, in the middle of this chaos stands a miracle: the oldest restaurant in Hollywood. Since 1919, Musso & Frank has been serving Hollywood royalty, from writers such as Bukowski and Fitzgerald to clients so iconic that they're known by their first names only (*Mick, Keith, Marilyn, Johnny* or *Leo* to name just a few). Today the restaurant's legendary red booths and wooden panels make you feel like you're entering a time machine, a relic of a bygone era.

What makes this space special are the bartenders that have been there for decades; they wear their jackets red and serve their martinis strong, along with a "sidecar" (a little cup on the side to refill your glass). Just like that, Hollywood becomes a little more bearable.

MUSSO & FRANK GRILL
6667 HOLLYWOOD BLVD,
LOS ANGELES, CA 90028

+1 (323) 467-7788 | Instagram: @mussoandfrankgrill | mussoandfrank.com

Cocktails
EXIT

Cocktails
EXIT

Musso & Frank
Grill
Since 1919
OLDEST IN HOLLYWOOD
CATS
CATS
FEB 26–MAR 24
PANTAGES

Chengdu
Taste

#12

THE RESTAURANT THAT INVENTED A DISH THAT HAS **BEEN COPIED EVERYWHERE, EVEN IN CHINA**

To check out one of our favorite restaurants in LA, head over to the San Gabriel Valley's Chinese ethnoburb. The Sichuan spice is unlike its Thai or Mexican counterparts. It's more numbing than fiery and can prove quite addictive. Chengdu Taste is credited for having put the famously spicy food from this Chinese province on the map.

The restaurant invented a dish that has been copied everywhere – even in China! – called the toothpick lamb, which is a must have. We also recommend you order their boiled fish. In the words of the late, great food writer Jonathan Gold: "The taste flits around your lips and tongue with the weird vibrancy of a flashing Las Vegas sign."

You can't make a reservation and the lines can get very long. The best time to go is during the week – ideally just before closing which has the added advantage of less traffic on the way there.

CHENGDU TASTE
828 W VALLEY BLVD,
ALHAMBRA, CA 91803

No reservations, walk-in only
+ 1 (626) 588-2284

Cash only

JUMBO'S CLOWN ROOM
5153 HOLLYWOOD BLVD,
LOS ANGELES, CA 90027

+1 (323) 666-1187	Instagram: @jumbosclownroom	jumbos.com

#13

THE POLE-DANCING CLUB WHERE **COURTNEY LOVE MET KURT COBAIN**

It's impossible to dissociate Hollywood from Rock 'n' Roll. Jumbo's Clown Room is designed to celebrate just how much these two worlds intertwine. The room is a legendary musicians' haunt. It's a tiny bar with seriously skilled, badass pole dancers (but don't expect any nudity or striptease), dancing to rock and indie music hits by such greats as Radiohead, Queens of the Stone Age, and Led Zeppelin.

Legend has it that Courtney Love used to work here as a dancer and met Kurt Cobain when he came to the bar one night.

marilyn
Présenté et commenté par
ROCK HUDSON
FRANK SINATRA
SAMMY DAVIS JR.
DEAN MARTIN
PETER LAWFORD
ANGIE DICKINSON

#14

THE SHOP **FOR MOVIE FANS**

The movie industry was the second Californian gold rush and continues to propel the growth of Los Angeles today. This tiny bookstore has a wonderful selection of old movie posters, photographs, screenplays and books, all focused on Tinseltown. It was opened in 1938 and now stocks around 20,000 books and half a million photographs.

Thanks to all these books, you'll have a chance to fine-tune your movie knowledge – plus you can meet actors and screenwriters at the talks and book signings held at the shop.

LARRY EDMUNDS BOOKSHOP
6644 HOLLYWOOD BLVD,
LOS ANGELES, CA 90028

+1 (323) 463-3273 | Instagram: @larryedmunds1938 | larryedmunds.com

#15

WANDER AROUND **A BREATHTAKING GARDEN**

California's turn-of-the-(last)-century boom owes a lot to one of the richest men of his era, Henry E. Huntington, who helped develop the railroad there.

In Pasadena, you can visit his magnificent villa and, in particular, its sublime gardens. Encompassing some 120 acres – including a Chinese Garden, Desert Garden, Japanese Garden with its gorgeous collection of bonsai, Rose Garden, Herb Garden, and Shakespeare Garden – it's so vast you probably won't manage to explore it all in just one day.

Huntington's own fine art collection is scattered in buildings throughout the property and includes great 18th-century English portraits, American and European art, letters, manuscripts and rare books, with a particular emphasis on science.

THE HUNTINGTON LIBRARY, ART COLLECTIONS, AND BOTANICAL GARDENS
1151 OXFORD RD, SAN MARINO, CA 91108

+1 (626) 405-2100 | huntington.org

IN-N-OUT

#16

EAT YOUR BURGER **THE CALIFORNIAN WAY**

Despite its healthy reputation, it was Los Angeles that invented the fast-food burger restaurant, a natural fit with the city's car-forward culture. McDonald's can certainly take credit for exporting this idea, but In-N-Out Burger is the chain that has won the hearts and stomachs of LA locals, critics, and chefs alike.

Unlike McDonald's, which famously uses franchises, In-N-Out Burger owns all its restaurants and maintains high quality standards, including the fact that the meat is never frozen.

At any time, day or night, you can find an endless line of cars waiting at In-N-Out's drive-throughs, while their competitors nearby remain empty. But so you don't end up looking like a burger bumpkin, we recommend respecting the fine art of ordering right (see next page).

IN-N-OUT BURGER
7009 SUNSET BLVD,
LOS ANGELES, CA 90028
(and many other locations)

No reservations, walk-in only

in-n-out.com

THE SECRET MENU AT IN-N-OUT

In-N-Out is known and celebrated for its simple offering: burgers, fries, soda, and shakes. That's it. But you would seriously miss out if we didn't tell you something that every Californian already knows: they have an extensive "secret" menu that you can also find online. Here are some of the most requested ones:

"Double double animal style": 2 patties, 2 cheese slices, animal style (with their signature burger spread made from mayonnaise, ketchup, relish, and vinegar) with caramelized onions.

"Fries animal style": fries with 2 melted cheese slices on top with animal-style spread and caramelized onions.

"Neapolitan shake": milkshake with chocolate, vanilla, and strawberry flavors mixed.

"Grilled cheese": sandwich with two slices of cheese and optional add-ons such as spread, tomatoes, lettuce, chopped chilies, and onions.

"Protein burger": with lettuce leaves instead of a bun.

Quality you can taste
DOUBLE-DOUBLE
CHEESEBURGER
HAMBURGER
FRENCH FRIES
Always Fresh
Ordering as easy as
1
Double-Double, French Fries, and Medium Drink
$7.75
2
IN-N-OUT
available
upon
request

#17

THE SECRET MALIBU BEACH **YOU CAN ONLY ACCESS AT LOW TIDE**

While Malibu may have the most beautiful beaches in the LA region, some of its wealthy residents wish they could keep them off limits to more ordinary mortals.

This stretch of coastline is where Malibu really started, where movie stars began snatching up quiet, picturesque houses creating "the Malibu movie colony" in the 1930s. It's a dreamy, rather unvisited setting, so it may feel like you have the Malibu beach all to yourself.

But be warned! You can only access this part of the beach at low tide. The high tide closes the exits at both ends, starting 2 hours before peak tide, so please plan accordingly. You will not be able to exit or access if you don't check the Malibu tides online beforehand. For parking, we recommend Malibu Lagoon car park. From there, walk until you're on the beach; once you see the houses, turn right along the beach and voilà – you're there! You can stop for lunch at Malibu Farm Pier Cafe before or after, a charming restaurant on the waterfront.

COLONY BEACH
MALIBU LAGOON CAR PARK,
CROSS CREAK ROAD, MALIBU, CA 90265

FREE

Only go at low tide!
Check Malibu tides time online: : tide-forecast.com

Asian Pears
$3.00/lb

#18

SHOP FOR YOUR PRODUCE **WITH LOCAL CHEFS**

If you want to understand why California is the envy of chefs around the world, just go to Santa Monica on a Wednesday and Saturday mornings: the farmers market showcases a huge array of high quality local fruits and vegetables, all thriving in the SoCal sunshine.

Wander around, marvel at the colors and smells. Los Angeles will feel different if you can enjoy the produce not only in restaurants. Some of our favorite stands are: Flora Bella Farm, Peads and Barnett, Mike & Sons Egg Ranch, Kenter Canyon Farms, Wild Local Seafood, J.J's Lone Daughter Ranch, and Harry's Berries.

If for some reason you can't make it, the Sunday farmers market in Hollywood is almost as good.

SANTA MONICA'S FARMERS MARKET
ARIZONA AVE AND 2ND STREET,
SANTA MONICA, CA 90401

Markets on Wednesday and Saturday mornings

Creative Office Space
Randy Starr
310.899.1800
Foot Locker
JUICE

#19

THE BEST SUSHI IN TOWN **IN AN UNUSUAL SPOT**

Between the freeway, an aging adult store and a rusty welding shop, possibly the best sushi in town can be found. Chef Shunji helped Chef Nobu start Matsuhisa in 1987 (the first "Nobu"). After going back to Japan, he returned to LA and opened Shunji in 2012, garnering many awards.

The place may feel casual but the food is very traditionally Japanese (they fly their fish in from Japan). Don't ask for mayo-filled Californian rolls or spicy tuna. And you won't need soy sauce or extra wasabi, the sushi is served perfectly seasoned. The best way to enjoy the menu is "Omakase" ("I'll leave it up to you"), in other words, in the expert hands of the chef.

And here's an added bonus: check out the shape of the building, a prime example of "novelty" or "programmatic" architecture, shaped to mimic its function. Before serving sushi, the locale used to be a Chili Bowl fast food joint and it looks just like the kind of bowl chili con carne is typically served in.

SHUNJI
3003 OCEAN PARK BLVD
SANTA MONICA, CA 90405

+1 (310) 826-4737
Instagram: @shunjijapanesecuisine

Reservations highly recommended

exploretock.com/shunji

HOTEL

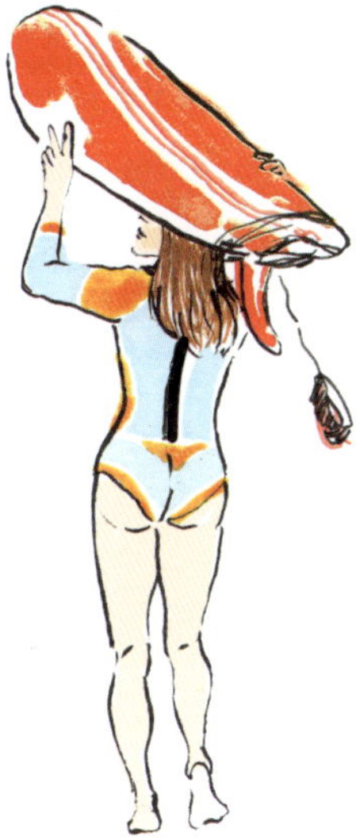

#20

THE HOTEL NEXT TO **YOUR SURF SPOT**

Just a stone's throw from the Pacific, the Gjelina Hotel offers its guests a wealth of options: excellent restaurants (part of the Gjusta/Gjelina group), a morning jog along the beach, a bike ride or a surf session ...

You could almost forget you're in the middle of a sprawling city.

Created by fashion photographer Glen Luchford, the hotel was later bought by the Gjelina group, who decorated the rooms in a minimalist-hippie-Venice Beach style that's both chic and

GJELINA HOTEL
15 ROSE AVE,
VENICE, CA 90291

+1 (323) 515 1215

Online booking only: gjelinahotel.com

frontdesk@gjelinahotel.com
Instagram: @gjelinahotel

LOS ANGELES
HOTELS

CHATEAU MARMONT

WEST HOLLYWOOD

Rock & roll rooms & bungalows

SHUTTERS ON THE BEACH

SANTA MONICA

East coast chic right on the sand

ACE HOTEL

DOWNTOWN LA

Historic hip hotel with fairly good value

THE HOLLYWOOD ROOSEVELT

HOLLYWOOD

Hockney-painted pool and Hollywood mischief

#21

THE JAZZ BAR **CREATED BY MUSIC ROYALTY**

The understated Vibrato Grill Jazz club is hidden away in the Los Angeles hills, inside a Mulholland Drive strip mall. This place was created by "music royalty" Herb Alpert, the trumpet player who sold more records than The Beatles in 1966. He also founded the record label A&M, which discovered Cat Stevens, Supertramp, The Police, and The Carpenters.

This intimate club has tiny dinner tables and incredible acoustics – no expense was spared. You can see a Beverly Hills crowd cheering at regular performances by the master himself or by his friends such as Seth MacFarlane, creator of Family Guy and a great Sinatra fan who regularly performs covers of the iconic crooner with his original band.

VIBRATO GRILL JAZZ
2930 BEVERLY GLEN CIR,
LOS ANGELES, CA 90077

Shows most days of the week

See website for updated calendar and reservations: vibratogrilljazz.com +1 (310) 474-9400

Bar or table reservation sometimes with cover charge

YAMAHA
Vibrato

22

JAMES TURRELL'S **GALLERY**

Los Angeles may be teeming with artists and galleries, but only one of them is 100% the brainchild of the legendary James Turrell, famous for his exceptional light installations and celebrity fans, including Drake and Kanye West.

The gallery houses pieces by many other great artists such as David Lynch, Peter Shire, and Ken Price. But the gallery is a piece of art in itself. When you visit, ask to see their meeting room, a Turrell Skyspace with a retractable ceiling which is magical around sunset.

PACE GALLERY
1201 SOUTH LA BREA AVE,
LOS ANGELES, CA 90019

FREE

+1 (310) 586-6886

pacegallery.com/galleries/los-angeles
Instagram: @pacegallery

GENERAL STORE

#23

THE SHOP THAT EMBODIES **THE VENICE BEACH LIFESTYLE**

This is the place to find the perfect Venice Beach souvenir. The store, opened in 2012 by couple Hannah Henderson and John Moore, celebrates Californian makers at their finest.

It offers a selection of well-curated books, ceramics, denim, dresses, jewels, magazines, vintage books, terrariums, and posters. Most of what is sold is made locally and picked for its high quality.

VENICE GENERAL STORE
1801 LINCOLN BLVD,
VENICE, CA 90291

+1 (310) 751-6393 | Instagram: @generalstore | shop-generalstore.com

MARISCOS
JALISCO

#24

JONATHAN GOLD'S **FAVORITE TACO TRUCK**

It's impossible to talk about Los Angeles food without mentioning Jonathan Gold, who was the first food critic to win a Pulitzer Prize. Gold passed in 2018, but the documentary made shortly before his death, *City of Gold*, gives an excellent insight into Gold's life and work and the LA food scene that he so loved. He had an affection for hard-to-reach restaurants and "honest" cooking by immigrants looking to add their traditions to this multicultural city.

Gold's favorite taco truck was Mariscos Jalisco. The city's ties with Mexico are very strong and with so many Mexicans working and living here the taco has become one of LA's official foods.

You can grab a taco East of Downtown, in a random, mostly residential location where Chef Raul Ortega has been parking his food truck since the 1980s. He specializes in fresh seafood, with his signature dish being the unforgettable "tacos dorados de camaron", shrimp tacos in a crunchy shell with avocado and salsa.

MARISCOS JALISCO
3040 E OLYMPIC BLVD,
LOS ANGELES, CA 90023

+1 (323) 528-6701 | mariscosjalisco.net | Cash only

Jonathan Gold

Jonathan Gold was a Pulitzer Prize-winner food critic who tirelessly covered the massive Los Angeles restaurant scene for the *Los Angeles Times* and *LA Weekly*. We did this interview just a few weeks before he sadly passed away in summer 2018.

It seems that you're very interested in restaurants that are country-specific, on the cheaper side, and slightly out of the way, maybe in strip malls?

Yeah. One of the things that makes Los Angeles an interesting food city, unlike most others, is that the barriers between high and low don't exist as much as they do in most places. That you have a place like Guerrilla Tacos, for instance. The chef, Wes Avila, has a haute-cuisine background. He studied with Alain Ducasse. He worked at your high-end restaurants here, and decided to go off and do his own thing. But he has relationships with suppliers – he gets the best sea urchins and the best vegetables, and the best meat from people that everybody wishes they could get pork from. But instead of serving it on a $150 tasting menu, he's serving it on a taco and charging $7 for it. And people complain, "Wait, this taco costs $7?!" And you want to say, "You don't understand!" [Laughs]

I'd rather eat in Los Angeles than anywhere else in the world

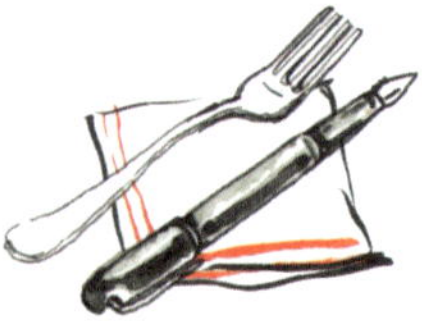

Do you think LA is one of the greatest cities in the world right now for food?

We don't have that many restaurants at the very, very top expensive level as New York would have, or Paris or Copenhagen. But I'd rather eat in Los Angeles than anywhere else in the world.

What would you say are some of the iconic dishes of Los Angeles?
Wow! What would you say? Would a Kogi taco be one of them? We're still in the middle of the avocado toast. You can roll your eyes at it, but it's still everywhere. And the thing is, it's everywhere in the world by now. But our avocados are better, and our bread is really fucking good. There's a Sichuan dish called Toothpick Lamb. And it doesn't exist in Sichuan, of course. A guy did it here. It's basically a nice, spicy cumin lamb dish. But they stick toothpicks in it so you can eat it as finger food.

And finally, besides food, what's great here?
I love the people and the ease of life, of course. I love the fact that, especially where I live in the city, I'm only 10-minutes' drive from a national forest with steep hills and plunging rivers and forests and things that you absolutely don't expect to have so close to the big city. I think Los Angeles is a place where you can be whoever you want to be. You can come from someplace else, make up the person that you want to be, and boom, you're that person! In the way that you can walk down some blocks in neighborhoods like Beverly Hills or Pasadena, and there'll be a Craftsman house alluding to 19th-century Japan, you'll see a Spanish hacienda, you'll see an Italian villa, you'll see a Tudor house, and they're all together on the block, and somehow it seems to fit.

#25

THE KOREAN SPA
OPEN 24/7

LA has the second-largest Korean population of any city, beaten only by Seoul. Large numbers of people migrated to the city following the Korean War in the 1950s. For blocks and blocks in LA's Koreatown, shops, street signs and billboards are written only in Korean.

In the midst of it, there is Wi Spa. It is a gigantic spa expanding over five floors (see the instructions on the next page). Suddenly you forget about time and space. The best part? It's open 24/7.

WI SPA
2700 WILSHIRE BLVD,
LOS ANGELES, CA 90057

Open 24/7	+1 (213) 487-2700 Instagram: @wispa_usa	wispausa.com

HOW
TO WI SPA

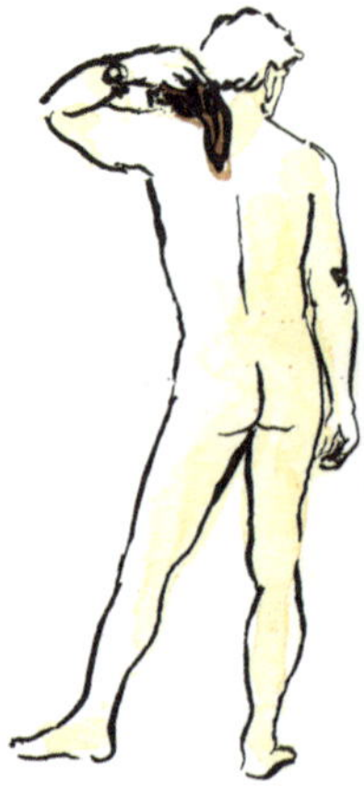

When you arrive, you're handed a towel, a t-shirt, and a locker-room magnetic key to wear at your wrist

Go undress in the respective locker rooms (Korean spas are always naked)

WI SPA

There is a co-ed space with a 24/7 restaurant, more saunas, nap areas, computers, and books

Here the Wi Spa uniform (short and t-shirt) is mandatory

Men and women have their own floors
with baths, showers, saunas, and resting rooms

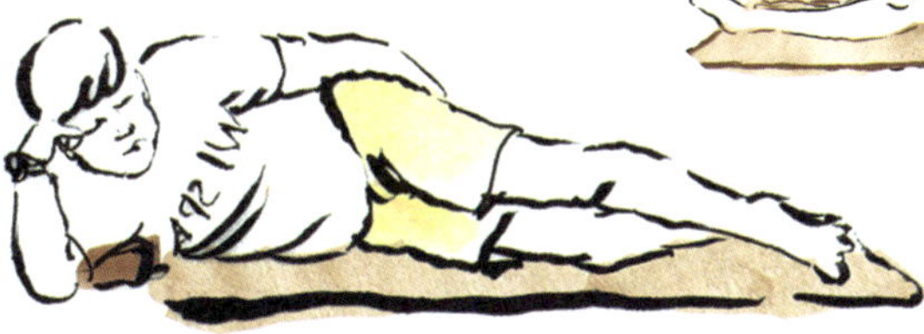

Treatments can be booked
ahead: the beloved scrubs,
massages, or manicures.
The upper floor is a terrace
to rest or tan

#26

THE MOVIE STAR
BUILDING

You have probably seen this building in movies such as *Blade Runner* and *The Artist*. The Bradbury Building is a movie star in its own right and one of the oldest in Los Angeles.

The building was designed by a young architect, George Wyman. An avid sci-fi reader, he was inspired by a novel that imagined workspaces organized around crystal courtyards.

Legend has it that Wyman only accepted the project because he received a message from his dead brother during an occult spiritualist session that said: "Take the Bradbury assignment. It will make you famous."

BRADBURY BUILDING
304 S BROADWAY,
LOS ANGELES, CA 90013

#27

THE BREAKFAST PLACE **WITH THE FAMOUS TAKE-HOME JAM**

Fruit jams can be incredibly comforting. The fruity, sweet flavor can be especially rewarding in the middle of winter, when you are in need of the taste of summer. That's exactly how Sqirl started, with chef Jessica Koslow making jams and designer Scott Barry handling the packaging. Their creations make the ideal gift to bring back from your trip to remind you of the Californian sunshine.

Since then, Koslow and Barry have created a fabulous brunch place, Sqirl, which offers some of the most addictive pastries, toasts, salads and bowls. The perfect Los Angeles brunch.

SQIRL
720 N VIRGIL AVE #4,
LOS ANGELES, CA 90029

No reservations, walk-in only +1 (323) 284-8147	Instagram: @sqirlla	sqirlla.com

SQIRL

California didn't invent the avocado toast but it certainly made it famous. And Sqirl definitely has one of the best versions around. If you don't believe us, just check out the restaurant's daily lines – proof that they've understood "Everything [we] Want to Eat" (the title of their cookbook).

– JESSICA KOSLOW –

CHEF AND CO-FOUNDER OF SQIRL

How did you get into cooking jams?

I'm from LA and left when I was 18 to be a pastry chef in Atlanta. In the South, preservation is so important (charcuterie, pickles) because the seasons are short and there is little time for the good stuff. I moved back to LA when I was 28 and I started a jam company with my boyfriend at the time, Scott Barry, in 2010.

It's truly a city that embraces the flavors of people

What's the Californian fruit you're most excited about?

Oh my god, that's a big question! There are a few: Blenheim apricots are my all-time favorites! I cannot wait for Gravenstein apples or Santa Rosa plums to come back.

What do you love about Los Angeles?

So much! How dynamic it is. It's truly a city that embraces

the flavors of people.
It can be Mexican, it can be Thai, it can be all of these things. It's inviting.

What's your favorite secret gem of a place in LA?

I love Bonjuk: it's a restaurant in Koreatown doing juk (Korean porridge), it's super weird. I love Tire Shop Taqueria. I love Sapp Coffee Shop. The "hole in a wall" spots.

How does your ideal day off look like in LA?

I don't ever have a day off!
But it would be going to Wi Spa, working out with yoga or Soul-Cycle, which is my jam. Finding a good gallery. Eating Japanese food at restaurants like Asanebo to pamper myself. I love to go out with my friends to the Gold Line bar and get a drink – spending time with people I love is really important.

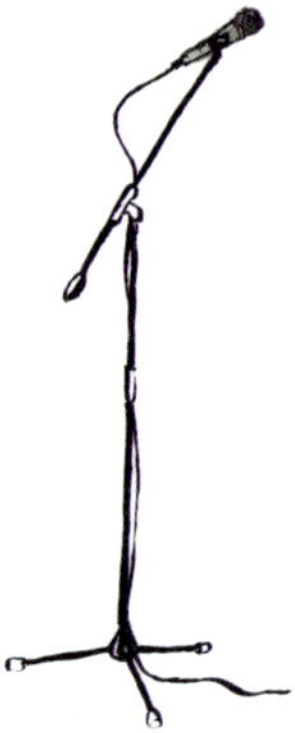

#28

THE SMALLEST COMEDY CLUB **FOR THE BIGGEST ACTS**

It's a good idea to have a strategy if you want to experience Largo at the Coronet, a remarkably intimate venue. Book ahead on their website, show up early to leave your name at the door, get your ticket and seat number (the earlier you come, the closer to the stage you sit), have dinner across the street at Aburiya Raku, and come back for the 8:30pm show.

Some of the best nights are the benefits or the "... and friends" shows, where a confirmed standup brings three to five other comedians and a musical guest for an old-school, music-hall type of show, often filled with surprises.

With fewer than 300 seats, it's a treat to see up-and-coming comedians mingling with Hollywood royalty such as: Zach Galifianakis, Will Ferrell, Adam Sandler, Sacha Baron Cohen, Ellen De Generes, Jeff Goldblum, Jack Black, Judd Apatow, and many more.

LARGO AT THE CORONET
366 N LA CIENAGA BLVD,
LOS ANGELES, CA 90048

Shows most days of the week

See website for updated calendar and reservations:
largo-la.com

at the
Coronet
and
the Little Room
www.largo-la.com

#29

BUY A VINYL AND A DRESS **FROM THE SAME YEAR**

Started by Carmen Hawk, a former award-winning fashion designer with experience in magazine covers, this vintage clothing shop has a true cult following. She's known to have an eye for expertly picking vintage clothing across many different eras and organizing all items by style and/or color.

She also sells close to 6,000 vinyl records a year, all handpicked with her partner Rodney Klein, who has a music background.

It's hard to leave the store without buying something, as prices are still affordable. This is partly due to the fact that the rent is cheap, being located in the Highland Park area, which has only recently seen an influx of restaurants and shops.

AVALON VINTAGE
106 N AVE 56,
LOS ANGELES, CA 90042

+1 (323) 309-7717

Instagram: @avalonvintage_records and @avalonvintage_clothing

OUTLETS
PRINCE
METALLICA
EXODUS
LOGAN'S RUN

AMAZING
ACTION!
2nd
Shocker!
COLOR
BIRTH
AT LAST
—I AM
FREE!
T. REX
KINKS
VELVET UNDERGROUND

© LAURE JOLIET

#30

ENJOY THAI "DRINK FOOD" **PAIRED WITH RARE NATURAL WINES**

As a teenager, chef Kris Yenbamroong spent many nights enjoying Thai "drink food" in the streets of Bangkok. His Night + Market Song restaurant elevates this cuisine while marrying it with European natural wines.

The result is an affordable, delicious, colorful, funny, sometimes experimental, loud restaurant. It offers bold flavors and unexpected organic wine pairings. It's ideal to go with a group of friends and share.

Of course, the restaurant has quickly become a favorite of both locals and visiting chefs. Interestingly, Yenbamroong is completely self-taught. He went to study film at NYU, and was working for photographer Richard Kern when his family asked him to take over their restaurant on Sunset Boulevard ... which he has reinvented successfully.

NIGHT + MARKET SONG
3322 SUNSET BLVD,
LOS ANGELES, CA 90026

No reservations, walk-in only

+1 (323) 665-5899
Instagram: @ntmrkt

nightmarketsong.com

© LAURE JOLIET

© EMILY KNECHT

In this collection, the last address won't always be revealed because it's too confidential. Up to you to find it!

31

NOT A BAD LAST TRICK **IN LOS ANGELES!**

Located in the Hollywood Hills, the Magic Castle Hotel is a fabulous secret club for magicians, open only to practitioners of the art and their friends. It's also the headquarters of the Academy of Magical Arts.

If you want to attend the de rigueur dinner show before getting lost in a castle full of secret passageways and magicians but don't personally know any, here's a tip: book a room at the Castle Hotel.

This has the added advantage that you won't have to get in your car after your third or fourth cocktail ...

MAGIC CASTLE

Very strict dress code: don't forget to pack "evening wear or business attire that is conservative, formal, and elegant"

You will not be able to get in unless you have a pass

Magic
Castle

340

© DANE DEANER – UNSPLASH

MANY THANKS TO

FANY PÉCHIODAT for her contagious enthusiasm and support on this project (and the wonderful Fabrice Nadjari for introducing us).

PIA RIVEROLA and CLARA MARI for their beautiful art that brings to life these experiences.

THOMAS JONGLEZ for this great collection of guide books.

OLIVIER ZAHM and BRAD ELTERMAN for letting us use the Jonathan Gold interview we did together.

BILLIE WEISMAN for welcoming us into her house.

JESSICA KOSLOW for her time and generosity in all she does.

JOEL CHEN, BIANCA CHEN and ANNA CARADEUC for their passion.

STEVE TURNER and ANTOINE CHOUSSAT for being the first to encourage me to talk about what's behind the LA doors.

JONATHAN GOLD for inspiring all of us to explore more.

© MIKA WEGELIUS – UNSPLASH

This book was created by:
André Michel, author
Pia Riverola, photographer
Clara Mari, illustrator
Emmanuelle Willard Toulemonde, layout
Jana Gough, Alice Mahoney and Charlotte Taschen, editing
Kimberly Bess and Bettina Bullimore, proofreading
Sophie Schlondorff and Olivia Fuller, additional translation
Mado de La Quintinie, publishing

You can write to us at info@editionsjonglez.com
Follow us on Instagram on @jonglez_publishing

Photo cover: Justin Choi – Pexels

Jonathan Gold interview initially published by *Purple Magazine* in September 2018.
THANK YOU

From the same publisher

Photo Books

Abandoned America: The age of Consequences
Abandoned Asylums
Abandoned Australia
Abandoned Belgium
Abandoned Churches: Unclaimed Places of Worship
Abandoned Cinemas of the World
Abandoned France
Abandoned Germany
Abandoned Lebanon
Abandoned Italy
Abandoned Japan
Abandoned Spain
Abandoned USSR
Abandoned World – An AI-generated exploration
After the Final Curtain: The Fall of the American Movie Theater
After the Final Curtain: America's Abandoned Theaters
Baikonur – Vestiges of the Soviet Space Program
Cinemas – A French Heritage
Chernobyl's Atomic Legacy – 25 years after disaster
Clickbait – A visual journey through AI-generated stories
Destination: Wellness – Our 35 best places in the world to take time out
Forbidden Places – Exploring our Abandoned Heritage
Forgotten Heritage
Oblivion
Parisian Theatres – Exceptional Venues
Secret Art Nouveau
Secret Sacred Sites
The cinemas of India – An exceptional heritage
Venice deserted
Venice from the skies

"Confidential" and "Soul of" Guides

Berlin Confidential
Lisbon Confidential
Malta Confidential
Marrakesh Confidential
Munich Confidential
New York Condential
Paris Confidential

Soul of Amsterdam - A guide to the 30 best experiences
Soul of Athens – 30 experiences
Soul of Barcelona – 30 experiences
Soul of Brussels – A guide to exceptional experiences
Soul of Detroit – A guide to exceptional experiences
Soul of Kyoto – A guide to exceptional experiences
Soul of Marseille – A guide to exceptional experiences
Soul of Milan – A guide to exceptional experiences
Soul of Rome – A guide to exceptional experiences
Soul of Tokyo – A guide to exceptional experiences
Soul of Venice – A guide to exceptional experiences
Soul of Vienna – A guide to exceptional experiences

Atlases of curiosities

Atlas of extreme weather
Atlas of forbidden places
Atlas of geographical curiosities
Atlas of geographical curiosities – Britain
Atlas of unusual wines
Atlas of urban vineyards

Secret atlases

Berlin – The secret atlas
London – The secret atlas
New York – The secret atlas
Paris – The secret atlas
Rome – The secret atlas
Venice – The secret atlas

"Secret" Guides

Secret Amsterdam
Secret Bali – An unusual guide
Secret Bangkok
Secret Barcelona
Secret Bars & Restaurants in Paris
Secret Bath – An unusual guide
Secret Belfast
Secret Berlin
Secret Boston – An unusual guide
Secret Brighton – An unusual guide
Secret Brooklyn
Secret Brussels
Secret Budapest
Secret Buenos Aires
Secret Campania
Secret Cape Town
Secret Copenhagen
Secret Corsica
Secret Dolomites
Secret Dublin – An unusual guide
Secret Edinburgh – An unusual guide
Secret Florence
Secret French Riviera
Secret Geneva
Secret Glasgow – An unusual guide
Secret Granada
Secret Helsinki
Secret Istanbul
Secret Johannesburg
Secret Kuala Lumpur
Secret Lisbon
Secret Liverpool – An unusual guide
Secret London – An unusual guide
Secret London – Unusual Bars & Restaurants
Secret Los Angeles – An unusual guide
Secret Louisiana
Secret Madrid
Secret Mexico City
Secret Milan
Secret Montreal – An unusual guide
Secret Naples
Secret New Orleans – An unusual guide
Secret New York – An unusual guide
Secret New York – Curious Activities
Secret New York – Hidden Bars & Restaurants
Secret Normandy
Secret Paris
Secret Potsdam
Secret Prague
Secret Provence
Secret Rio
Secret Rome
Secret Seville
Secret Singapore
Secret Stockholm
Secret Strasbourg
Secret Sussex – An unusual guide
Secret Tokyo
Secret Tuscany
Secret Venice
Secret Venice Lagoon
Secret Vienna
Secret Washington DC – An unusual guide
Secret York – An unusual guide

In accordance with regularly upheld French jurisprudence (Toulouse 14-01-1887), the publisher will not be deemed responsible for any involuntary errors or omissions that may subsist in this guide despite our diligence and verifications by the editorial staff.

Registration of copyright: September 2026 – Edition: 01
ISBN: 978-2-38715-079-0
Printed in July 2026, by Dedrax, Bulgaria

Negative Capability